TOP CAR
RECORDS

THE ULTIMATE GUIDE TO THE FASTEST, COOLEST AND CRAZIEST CARS EVER!

CONOR KILGALLON

Book Fairs
Book Clubs
SCHOLASTIC

THIS IS A CARLTON BOOK

Published in Great Britain in 2014 by
Carlton Books Limited
20 Mortimer Street
London W1T 3JW

A CIP catalogue for this book is available from the British Library.

ISBN 978-1-78312-107-6

Jacket design: James Pople
Production: Rachel Burgess
Picture research: Steve Behan
Packager: Conor Kilgallon

Printed and bound in China

10 9 8 7 6 5 4 3 2 1

For Calum and Freya

Previous page: Ferrari LaFerrari. Opposite: SSC Tuatara.
Page 4: Porsche 911 GT2 RS and Hennessey Venom GT.
Page 5: Bugatti Veyron Super Sport and Ferrari LaFerrari.

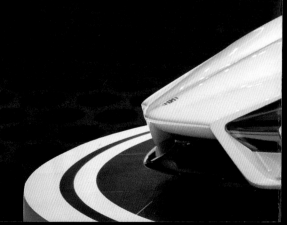

CONTENTS

INTRODUCTION

Cars, cars, brilliant cars. Part of everyone's daily lives, they're everywhere, from crowded city streets to the most remote jungle tracks. And everyone has their own opinion on what makes a good one. Whatever your favourites are, cars are made up of more than just a set of numbers. Sure, top speed, horsepower and acceleration are important but driving is thrilling and fun and the very best cars are the ones that manage to make you love them by mixing speed, handling and style in just the right amounts.

In this book you'll find the fastest, the smallest, the most famous, the most beautiful, the most inventive, and just the plain craziest cars ever made, past and present, all of which will make your heart race or your head pound – or both. Some you'll recognize straight away and some you may never have heard of.

But whether it's the original Benz Motorwagen or the lightning fast Bugatti Veyron, the tiny Peel P50 or the massive Marauder, the bestselling Beetle or the most exclusive Rolls-Royce, all of the cars on the pages that follow will grab your attention and make you gasp at the creative and technological capabilities that each different amazing automobile has to offer.

THE FIRST CARS

Compared to today's super-quick and glamorous turbo machines, the world's first cars are pretty ordinary. But, at the time, they were a revolution. Giving the horse and carriage some well-deserved time off, the world's greatest technological pioneers designed a new mode of transport that was set to completely modernize the world.

BENZ PATENT-MOTORWAGEN (1886-93)

The internal combustion engine we all know today gradually came to life during the mid-19th century but the Benz Patent-Motorwagen was the first vehicle to be specifically designed to be powered by one. For this achievement it is known as the world's first automobile (to call it a car at this point in time would be stretching it a bit). Germans Karl Benz and his wife Bertha were the inventors of this amazing new three-wheeled machine with its rear-mounted engine, originally producing just $^2/_3$hp from its 954cc single-cylinder engine. The surname of this truly visionary pair lives on today in the name Mercedes-Benz.

The Benz Patent-Motorwagen was the world's first automobile.

ROLLS-ROYCE 10HP
(1904)

This beautiful little car is the oldest surviving Rolls-Royce model and is the machine that established the name of the company started by Charles Stewart Rolls and Frederick Henry Royce. Powered by a 1800cc water-cooled twin-cylinder engine the car actually produced 12hp and could fly along at 39mph (63km/h). Only 16 cars were made and, as was standard practice at the time, the car was sold as an engine and chassis only – customers had to get the bodywork designed by a separate coachbuilder. This model is so rare (it is one of only four in existence) that one sold at auction for £3.2 million ($5.4 million) in 2007.

This lovely 10hp model is the oldest surviving Rolls-Royce.

FORD MODEL T
(1908-27)

In just 22 years, the automobile progressed from the three-wheeled Benz Patent-Motorwagen of 1886 to Henry Ford's Model T. This famous car was the first to bring motoring within the reach of ordinary people by using production line techniques to keep costs down. But this was also an easy-to-drive, well-made car powered by a light, strong 2898cc four-cylinder engine. The car's popularity was so great that at the height of its fame, one Model T came off the production lines every 10 seconds. It eventually went on to sell more than 15 million cars around the world. The motor industry was never the same again.

New Model T cars being put together at Ford's factory in Manchester.

DESIGN CLASSICS

By the time the 1920s dawned, cars were starting to come of age. No longer just clunky, unreliable metal machines on wheels, the best (and most expensive) ones had become sleek, luxurious and fast.

BUGATTI TYPE 41 ROYALE (1927-33)

This was the era that made Ettore Bugatti's name famous and this was one of his best cars. Better known as the Royale, he planned to sell the model to royalty but the Great Depression took hold and killed off his dream. In the end, he only managed to sell six, each of which is so unique that it has its own name. Bugatti did not do things by halves when it came to building this car. It was enormous, the biggest of its time at 21ft (6.4m) long. It weighed an astonishing 3.2 tonnes (7,000lb), making it nearly 25 percent bigger and heavier than even the largest luxury cars today. Powered by a 12.7-litre eight-cylinder engine, it could produce up to 300bhp, making it colossal all round. With its long bonnet and sweeping lines is it also one of the most extravagant cars ever made.

The Royale was built for aristocrats and was one of the biggest cars of its day.

BUGATTI TYPE 57SC ATLANTIC (1934-40)

The Type 57 was another masterpiece, this time designed by Ettore Bugatti's son, Jean. Clearly a chip off the old block, Jean also knew how to design a beautiful car. One Type 57 model was the SC Atlantic, a coupé in the 'avant garde' style that matched the fashions of the time perfectly. Unusually, it had a raised seam running front to back, produced by external riveting. The original. The SC used a supercharged 3.3-litre eight-cylinder engine to produce 200bhp and a 120mph (190km/h) top speed. Just four were made and only two survive. One is owned by fashion designer Ralph Lauren and the other was sold at auction in 2010 for an undisclosed sum, thought to be in the region of a record-breaking £18–27 million ($30–40m), making this the most sought-after car in motoring history.

JAGUAR XK120 (1948-61)

This was Jaguar's first moment of triumph. The XK120 was a beauty to look at and had the performance to match. It was powered by a 3.4-litre XK unit that was so good it survived into the 1990s. Producing 160bhp from its 3.4-litre straight-six engine, it could reach 120mph (192km/h), which was just as well because that's why the car was called the XK120. At the time, it was the world's fastest production car. Even better, it wasn't particularly expensive and Jaguar just couldn't make them fast enough. Needless to say, a car this good was raced and rallied and was updated several times before being replaced by the famous E-Type. It's fair to say these were golden years for Jaguar.

HOT HYPERCARS

In order to squeeze into this elite category, hypercars must be aerodynamic, weigh next-to-nothing, go supremely fast and look as if they have been sent back from the future. These are – without a doubt – the fastest cars on the planet...

BUGATTI VEYRON SUPER SPORT (2005-)

The Veyron is the daddy, the car that put the 'hyper' in hypercar. The original version could hit 254mph (408km/h) via a 0–60mph (97km/h) time of 2.5 seconds, which was just ridiculous. Needless to say, it was a record top speed. And it did it using a quad-turbo 8-litre W16 engine that pushed out 1,001bhp and which needed ten different radiators to cope with the heat produced by the engine. And of course it had all-wheel drive and fantastic handling. But Bugatti weren't satisfied so in 2010, they revealed the Super Sport version, with 1,184bhp and an astonishing top speed of 267.86mph (431.07km/h), another record. This car will always be the benchmark against which all future performance cars are measured – the defining word in power, speed and technical brilliance.

The Veyron Super Sport is the world's fastest production car.

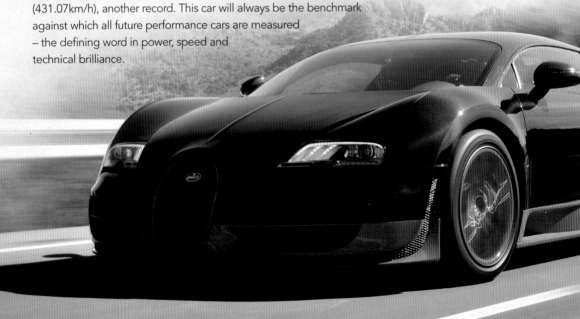

KOENIGSEGG AGERA R
(2011-)

Just when you thought it was all getting out of hand, along comes another amazing machine aiming for the 'fastest road car' title. This time it's one from Swedish company Koenigsegg. The Agera R is powered by a twin-turbo 5-litre V8 turning out an unbelievable 1,124bhp. This drives this lightweight carbon-fibre-everything masterpiece to a claimed 270mph (435km/h) and a 0–62mph (100km/h) time of 2.9 seconds, all handled with traction control systems and an electronically adjustable rear wing. We have lift-off!

The makers claim the Agera R has a top speed of 270mph (435km/h).

LAMBORGHINI AVENTADOR LP700-4
(2011-)

If it's a V12-engined Lamborghini, its going to be crazy, in a very good way. The Aventador was Lamborghini's replacement for the Murcielago and the styling had 'stealth fighter' written all over it. It was stunning in an old-school way – huge, low and wide and is actually the widest production car currently made at 80in (2m). Power comes from a 6.5-litre V12 producing 691bhp, and it handles brilliantly, in part due to its pushrod suspension, at the time unknown in a road car. And it is the fastest car Lamborghini had ever made. The top speed is claimed to be 217mph (350km/h), though it has been clocked at an even faster 230mph (370km/h).

The Aventador is the fastest car Lamborghini ever made.

PAGANI HUAYRA
(2012-)

Italian company Pagani does things its own way and this small company now produces the most desirable hypercars on the planet. The name Huayra is taken from the old Inca word for 'God of the Winds' – just about right for this car. Powering this sleekest of machines is a 720bhp Mercedes AMG twin-turbo 5.9-litre V12, with reworked engine-mapping to squeeze the last drop of performance out of it. All of which means its top speed is 231mph (372km/h), with a 0–60mph (97km/h) time of 3.2 seconds. And this is a hi-tech bit of kit. The Huayra uses carbotanium for its monocoque chassis, gullwing doors for posing appeal and active aerodynamics to keep the whole show on the road. And the sci-fi/steampunck interior has to be seen to be believed. For many, this was the outstanding performance car of 2012.

Pagani's 231mph (372km/h) Huarya was 2012's best hypercar.

GUMPERT APOLLO
(2005–12)

The ugliest supercar ever made? Well beauty is in the eye of the beholder and who cares anyway because this is all about performance. It's really a racing car adapted for the road and it's a cracker. 0–62mph (100km/h) comes up in 3.1 seconds, leading all the way to 224mph (360km/h). The engine behind this rocket ship is a twin-turbo 4.2-litre V8 pushing out 641bhp. Buy yourself the race version and that increases to a massive 789bhp, making it one of the most powerful petrol-driven road cars you can buy. Gumpert uniquely claim that at more that 190mph (306km/h), the downforce generated by the car is so great that the Apollo can be driven on the ceiling. But at £190,000 for the car, testing that out might be a bit risky.

HENNESSEY VENOM GT
(2012–)

The Venom GT is doing battle for the title of world's fastest road car with the Bugatti Veyron. And it has almost won. John Hennessey, the man behind the car, took a Lotus Exige and turned it into a rocket. If you thought the Veyron could pump out the horsepower, take a look at the Venom: 1,244bhp from a twin-turbo 7.0-litre V8 engine, taking the car from 0–60mph (97km/h) in 2.4 seconds and onto a claimed top speed of 270mph (447km/h).

The Venom GT claims a world record 270mph (435km/h) top speed.

The Apollo wasn't one the prettiest cars but it could hit 224mph (360km/h).

TRACK DAY FUN

Taking a fast car to a race track, where you can zoom around at any speed you like, has become the most fun you can have on four wheels. Several companies now make cars designed to offer a taste of single-seater racing while still being street-legal.

ARIEL ATOM 500 V8 (2011–)

Most cars have body panels but the Ariel Atom just has a cage. And a 500bhp 3.0-litre V8 engine, which in a car weighing just 550kg (1,213lb) (one of the lightest you can buy) gives a power-to-weight ratio of 909bhp per tonne. No other production car can boast this kind of figure, it is simply off the scale and means that the Atom will beat almost any car, except for the most extreme hypercars, around a normal racetrack. 0–60mph (97km/h) comes up in 2.3 seconds (making it the fastest accelerating car today) with a top speed of 168mph (269km/h). The only thing holding the car back is its price – at £140,000, this amazing thrills machine ain't cheap.

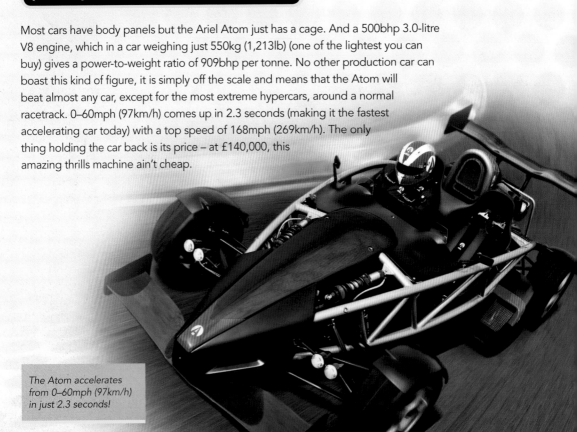

The Atom accelerates from 0–60mph (97km/h) in just 2.3 seconds!

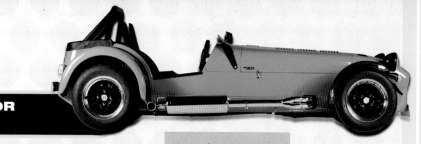

CATERHAM 7 620R
(2013-)

The performance from this Caterham 7 620R is completely off the scale.

2012 marked the 55th anniversary of the Caterham 7 (formerly the Lotus 7) but it still delivers fun and excitement by the bucket-load. Lightweight cars like these are all about their power-to-weight ratio and the 620R, the most bonkers of all current Caterham 7s, has some of the best figures in the business, turning out 568bhp per tonne from its 2.0-litre supercharged engine. Even the most exotic hypercars struggle to reach that kind of figure or match the lightning fast 0–60mph (97km/h) time of just 2.79 seconds. Hammer it down the straight and you can reach 155mph (248km/h), all in car that doesn't even have a windscreen or a roof, and still looks much the same as it did more than 50 years ago. This is a true track classic.

TOP 10
FASTEST ACCELERATING CARS (0–60MPH)

1	Ariel Atom 500 V8	2.3sec
2	Porsche 918	2.4sec
3	Bugatti Veyron Super Sport	2.46sec
4	Caparo T1	2.5sec
5	McLaren P1	2.6sec
6	Porsche 911 Turbo S	2.6sec
7	Lamborghini Aventador	2.7sec
8	SSC Ultimate Aero TT	2.8sec
9	Caterham 7 620R	2.79sec
10	BAC Mono	2.8sec

BAC MONO
(2011-)

The presence of headlights and number plates aren't fooling anyone – this is pure and simple a track-racing car. The driver sits in the middle of the car, uses an F3-spec sequential gearbox, an F1-inspired steering wheel and enjoys the best-balanced handling available to mankind. Power comes from a 2.3-litre four-cylinder Cosworth engine producing 285bhp, giving a magic power-to-weight ratio of 527bhp per tonne, 6bhp better than a Bugatti Veyron. All of this gives exquisite handling and performance, with 0–62 mph (100km/h) coming up in 2.8 seconds, and a top speed of 170mph (274km/h). No surprise then that it was highly praised when it came out.

The BAC Mono is the most sophisticated track car ever made.

RETRO CARS OF THE 1960s

The late 1950s and 1960s saw car design blossom. All the great manufacturers produced some of their best-looking cars during this period, many of which are now considered classics.

MERCEDES-BENZ 300SL (1954-63)

If Mercedes wasn't already famous enough, the 300SL (Sport Light) put the company in a totally different league. Yes, this was the car with the unique gullwing doors that made everyone drool. Underneath that low-profile bonnet lurked a beast of a motor. A 3-litre engine pushed out 240bhp, capable of taking the car all the way to 155mph (250km/h), making it the fastest car of its day. It was also the first car to use a fuel-injected engine. No one else was making anything like this at the time. It was a bit tricky to drive at high speed but that was quickly forgotten about and good examples of the car (1,850 were made) can now fetch more than $1 million (£600,000) at auction.

The 300SL was the world's fastest production car when it came out.

JAGUAR E-TYPE
(1961-75)

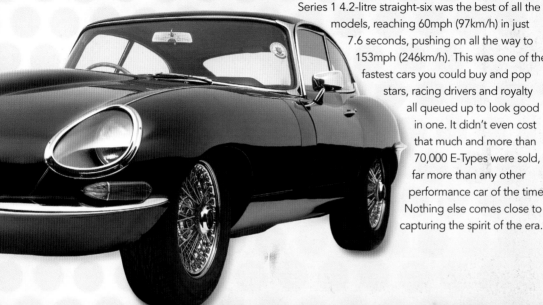

The stunning Jaguar E-Type was the 1960s wrapped up in a car.

The E-Type was the best performance car of the 1960s. Its stylish looks established the car as a true icon – many people believe it is the most beautiful car ever made. And it had the performance to back up its looks. The Series 1 4.2-litre straight-six was the best of all the models, reaching 60mph (97km/h) in just 7.6 seconds, pushing on all the way to 153mph (246km/h). This was one of the fastest cars you could buy and pop stars, racing drivers and royalty all queued up to look good in one. It didn't even cost that much and more than 70,000 E-Types were sold, far more than any other performance car of the time. Nothing else comes close to capturing the spirit of the era.

The AC Cobra was the fastest accelerating car of its time.

AC COBRA
(1962-68)

AC were a nice British company making pretty sports cars, like the Ace. Carroll Shelby was a Texan racer with a liking for big American V8 engines. Put the two together and you got the AC Cobra, a beast of a machine and one of the best examples of how a car can be utterly transformed. The Cobra started with a 4.7-litre V8 engine in it but that wasn't big enough for some people so a monstrous 7-litre V8 was then used instead. Needless to say, this made the car's performance stratospheric and in 1965, it was the fastest accelerating car in the world, reaching 60mph (97km/h) in just 4.2 seconds, before finally hitting 164mph (266km/h). With its flared wheelarches, racing stripes and pretty looks, it was the ultimate street racer.

FORD GT40
(1966-68)

The GT40 started life as a racing car, supposedly created to knock Ferrari off its perch in sports car racing. And it really succeeded, winning the Le Mans 24-Hour race four times in a row, giving Porsche a big scare as well. In its orange and blue Gulf Oil colours it was one of the most revered cars of its day – one sold at auction in 2012 for a whopping $11 million (£6.5 million), making it one of the most expensive auction cars ever. Just seven road-legal MkIII versions were made and powered by a 4.7-litre V8 producing 335bhp they could hit 164mph (262km/h) via a 0–60 (97km/h) time of six seconds. The '40' bit in the GT40's name refers to the car's height – just 40in (102cm). This was very low, which made getting in and out a bit tricky but nobody cared, lucky owners were buying a big bit of racing history.

Ford's rare GT40 could let you pretend to be a Le Mans racer.

LAMBORGHINI MIURA
(1966-72)

The Miura was a car from another planet. One of the most beautiful cars ever made, it was also a real rocket and established Lamborghini as the maker of the most advanced sports cars in the world. So it didn't just look great, it drove brilliantly, too. Power was from a 4-litre V12 producing up to 385bhp. It could reach 170mph (274km/h), an outrageous speed for its day, with 0–60mph (97km/h) coming up in a frantic 6.7 seconds. But its straight-line speed was only half the story. Because the engine was placed near the middle of the chassis, the car's balance and cornering ability was sublime. The greatest car of its day? It's hard to argue otherwise.

The most beautiful car ever? Many people think the Miura was perfect.

FERRARI DAYTONA (1968-73)

Ferrari no doubt had their feathers ruffled by Lambo's brilliant Miura, but no matter, they had their own beauty to show the world. The 365GTB/4 (to give it its full name) was named the Daytona in honour of Ferrari's victory in the famous US sports car race. Unlike the Miura, the Daytona was front-engined and a bit heavy so isn't considered such a brilliant 'driver's car', but it was very fast. Its 4.4-litre V12 pushed out 353bhp, meaning the car took just 5.4 seconds to reach 60mph (97km/h), with a Miura-baiting top speed of 174mph (278km/h). Its striking, muscular lines looked modern and this car has become one of the most collectable Ferrari's ever, helped in part by its appearances in TV programme *Miami Vice*.

TOP 10 FASTEST CARS OF THE 1950s AND 1960s

1	Ferrari Daytona	174mph (278km/h)
2	Lamborghini Miura	170mph (274km/h)
=	Maserati 5000 GT	170 mph (274km/h)
4	AC Cobra	164mph (266km/h)
=	Ford GT40 MkIII	164mph (262km/h)
6	Mercedes 300SL	155mph (250km/h)
=	Ferrari 410 Superamerica	155mph (250km/h)
8	Maserati Ghibli	154mph (248km/h)
9	Aston Martin DB4 GT Zagato	153mph (246km/h)
=	Jaguar E-Type	153mph (246km/h)

The Daytona is now one of the most sought-after Ferraris ever.

MUSCLE CARS

Built for speed, muscle cars perfectly showcase the golden age of the American motor industry, as well as the much-desired V8 engine. So put your foot on the gas, and let's take these powerful beauties out for a spin...

FORD MUSTANG BOSS 302 (1969-70)

The Mustang was the coolest car in America when it came out in 1964 and it was the muscle car to beat. It was one of the fastest-selling cars of all time, 418,000 units in its first year and a million sold by 1966. It has gone on to be Ford's longest-serving nameplate, along with the F-Series pick-up truck. And during its lifetime it just got faster and faster with a whole host of V8s pushing out more power. But a secret project, unofficially codenamed 'the boss's car', resulted in the mighty Boss 302. Originally developed for Trans Am road-racing the car had a 4.9-litre V8 officially producing 290bhp. This could propel the car to 60mph (97km/h) in 6.9 seconds, with a top speed of around 130mph (209km/h). And it was the fastest-looking Mustang of the lot with its 'hockey stick' stripes on the side and racing stripes on the bonnet.

The Mustang was a sensation in the 1960s and it still lives on today.

TOP 10 FASTEST ACCELERATING MUSCLE CARS 0–60MPH

1	1966 Chevrolet Corvette 427 – 4.8sec
2	1970 Chevrolet El Camino SS 454 – 5.0sec
3	1969 Ford Mustang Boss 429 – 5.1sec
4	1969 Plymouth Road Runner – 5.1sec
5	1969 Chevrolet Camaro ZL1 – 5.3sec
=	1971 Chevrolet Corvette ZR2 Stingray – 5.3sec
7	1970 Dodge Challenger R/T 426 – 5.4sec
8	1968 Chevrolet Corvette 427 – 5.5sec
=	1970 Buick GS Stage 1 455 – 5.5sec
10	1970 Plymouth Hemi Barracuda – 5.6sec

CBY 304G

CHEVROLET CAMARO Z28
(1970)

All the big American car companies wanted a piece of the Ford's success with the Mustang. Chevy's answer was the Camaro. It never really caught the imagination like the Mustang did, but it did manage to produce a genuine classic along the way – the Z28. This was a special edition, powered by a 5.7-litre V8 churning out 360bhp, which could launch the car to 60mph (97km/h) in 7.5 seconds and onto a top speed of over 120mph (193km/h). It also had sports suspension, front disc brakes, a rear spoiler, dual exhausts and the all-important go-faster stripes on the bonnet. Pony cars didn't go around corners very well, but this was different and was the best of the bunch.

The best of the 'pony cars'? The Camaro Z28 was loved then and now.

PLYMOUTH ROAD RUNNER SUPERBIRD
(1970)

Probably one of the most bizarre cars ever to take to the road, this winged wonder was one of the last of the pony cars. Really a road-car version of a NASCAR racer, the car was Plymouth's answer to the Dodge Charger Daytonas, Ford Torinos and Mercury Cyclones of the world. With its 'droop-snoot' nose and 'goalpost' rear spoiler it was every inch the oval-track racer. The most popular version of the lot was the terrifying-sounding Super Commando 440 V8, with a massive 7.2-litre V8, rated at 375bhp. This monster engine could hit 60mph (97km/h) in 5.5 seconds, really impressive for the time. The Superbird was a great success on the track but the road version only lasted a year. By the 2000s, they were among the most sought-after muscle cars at auction.

The Road Runner Superbird with its 'droop-snoot' and iconic spoiler.

HYPERHYBRIDS

Combining supercar speed with electric hybrid technology, hyperhybrids represent the new age of modern motoring combining both speed and efficiency. These are the cars of the future, now...

PORSCHE 918
(2013-)

Porsche really know a thing or two about making clever cars. After all, they rewrote the supercar rulebook with the electronically controlled 959 in the 1980s. Well, here's another cracker and this time its a hyperhybrid. And it's a beauty. As with all hybrids, power comes from a petrol engine and electric motor added together, in this case a full 887bhp from a 4.6-litre V8 delivering 608bhp, and two electric motors, which provide an extra 279bhp of whoompf. And as with anything electric, the power comes on so easily and quickly. Hitting the accelerator is like pressing a light switch, the power is just there, right away. The 918 hits 0–60mph (97km/h) in 2.4 seconds before going on to touch 214mph (345km/h), all of it delivered by four-wheel drive, four-wheel steer and computer-controlled-everything!

The 918 can hit 60mph (97km/h) in 2.4 seconds. Few cars are faster.

MCLAREN P1
(2013-)

1100

With over 900bhp on tap, the P1 is a massively powerful car.

Thought hybrid cars are all about saving the planet? Think again, because this one is all about racing around the planet as fast as possible. You see, the petrol part of the P1's engine is still a twin-turbo 3.8-litre V8 that delivers 727bhp. McLaren then added their own electric motor which by itself produces 176bhp for a combined output of an eye-watering 903bhp. 0–62mph (100km/h) comes up in 2.6 seconds and top speed is limited to 217mph (349km/h).

The LaFerrari's 950bhp powers the car to 218mph (351km/h).

FERRARI LAFERRARI
(2013-)

LaFerrari. *The* Ferrari, 'the chosen one'. Like the McLaren P1 and Porsche 918, this car represents everything Ferrari knows about making a fast car even faster by adding cutting-edge technology and electricity. At the car's heart is a 6.3-litre V12 which produces 789bhp, the most powerful normally aspirated production engine ever made. Add in some 'KERS' electrical assistance from an F1 car and you've got another 161bhp for a combined output of 950bhp, all of it going to the rear wheels. 0–62mph (100km/h) comes up in 2.9 seconds, before heading all the way to 218mph (351km/h). All 499 examples were bought before the car had even properly unveiled to the public.

COOL CONCEPTS

Driving around inside engineers' imaginations more than the nearest actual motorway, concept cars are a vision of the future. Designer Harley Earl popularized the idea of showing off prototype cars in the 1950s with his 'Motorama' travelling roadshow. Which one's your favourite?

FERRARI 512S MODULO (1970)

Pininfarina, the great Italian car design company, penned this one and unlike most concept cars, this futuristic wedge does actually go. Though not far, despite being based on Ferrari's famous 512S racing car, with its 5.0-litre V12 engine. The car has a canopy rather than doors (canopies are very popular in concept cars) that slides up and forwards to let the driver and a passenger in. A wonderful flight of fancy from a company that temporarily thought it was designing spaceships.

This striking concept car from Ferrari was designed by Pininfarina.

BMW GINA
(2001)

It's hard for a concept car to be any more experimental than the GINA because this isn't actually just one design, it's whatever you want it to be. After all, why limit yourself to old-fashioned rigid bodywork panels when you can have a shape-shifter? Where the bodywork should be is a moveable frame clad in seamless Spandex, a stretchable fabric usually found in cycling shorts. The driver can alter the shape of the frame and the Spandex just stretches to cover the new shape. OK, so there are a few hard panels otherwise the car would be more of a sail than a car but as for the rest, well, you decide. Grow a spoiler on Monday, flare your wheel arches on a Tuesday, get your headlights to wink on a Wednesday…

The GINA was unique. Why be stuck with just one body shape?

LAMBORGHINI EGOISTA
(2014)

Lamborghini, as you will see elsewhere in this book, is not a company that does things quietly. Their cars are as daring to look at as they are to drive and the Egoista is no different. Built to celebrate its 50th birthday, the car, based on the Gallardo model, has a 5.2-litre V10 engine pumping out 600bhp. Based on an existing model it may be but the attack-helicopter styling is in a world of its own – just look at that canopy, which is the only way in and out of the car (there is no need for anything as boring as a door). Dressed up entirely in aluminium and carbon fibre, it wouldn't be surprising to see this car jet off to carry out an airstrike.

From above, the Egoista is more jet fighter than car, with its canopy roof.

MEAN MACHINES OF THE 1970s

For car manufacturers, the 1970s were an uncertain decade. The 1973 oil crisis and global recession led to a sharp decline in car orders, all of which made car companies nervous and conservative, right? Well, sort of, but you'd never know from these designs.

LANCIA STRATOS (1972-74)

Back in the 1970s, Lancia was determined to win the World Rally Championship. It's weapon of choice? The Stratos. Gone were the curves of the 1960s and in came wedge shapes, and the Stratos was one serious wedge, winning in the Championship in 1974, 1975 and 1976. Rallying rules said that road-going versions of competition cars had to be made so the Stratos was unleashed on the public. Originally powered by a Ferrari Dino V6 engine, the car was as dramatic to drive as it was to look at, belting out over 140mph (224km/h), having reached 60mph (97km/h) in only five seconds. Less than 500 of Marcello Gandini's brilliant design were ever made but if you ever see one, you'll never forget it.

TOP 10

FASTEST CARS OF THE 1970s

1	Lamborghini Countach – 186mph (298km/h)	
2	Chevrolet Corvette Stingray – 170mph (274km/h)	
3	Monteverdi Hai – 169mph (272km/h)	
4	Lamborghini Urraco – 165mph (266km/h)	
5	BMW M1 – 164mph (265km/h)	
6	Porsche 911 Turbo – 162mph (261km/h)	
7	Lamborghini Jarama – 162mph (261km/h)	
8	DeTomaso Pantera – 160mph (256km/h)	
9	Maserati Bora – 160mph (256km/h)	
10	Ferrari 308 GTB – 155mph (249km/h)	

The Stratos was a thrilling design with true rally-winning abilities.

CORVETTE STINGRAY
(1968-84)

This was the second generation of this brilliant American car, which has gone on to be Chevrolet's longest-serving nameplate, along with the Camaro. When this 'new' shape appeared in 1968 it wasn't much liked but who knows, perhaps the unique atmosphere of the 1970s worked its magic because buyers started to flock to buy it. And it didn't just look great, with its pointy nose and Ferrari-style tail lights, it was very fast, too. The basic 5.7-litre V8 car could pump out 300bhp. If you opted for the massive 7.5-litre option, you had just bought yourself a 435bhp rocket, capable of 170mph (272km/h). In fact, the Stringray is so loved that it is still in production today, more than 50 years after it first appeared.

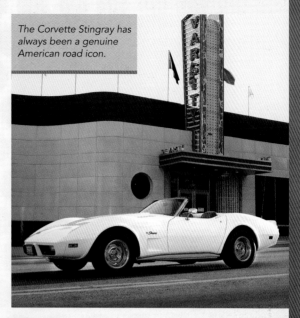

The Corvette Stingray has always been a genuine American road icon.

LAMBORGHINI COUNTACH
(1974-91)

If clothes in the 1970s were about flares, car design was about the wedge and Lamborghini, true to form, came up with something truly sensational. The Countach looked like it had just come off the set of a sci-fi movie, but it was real. Marcello Gandini, creator of the Lancia Stratos, also penned the Countach. It's fair to say he was on a roll. Powered by a 3929cc V12, the Countach was a 375bhp beast, roaring up to 186mph (298km/h), an astonishing speed at the time. Later versions had body kits, spoilers and a bigger engine, which either made the car look even more outrageous (a good thing) or tasteless (a bad thing), depending on your point of view. Whatever, few cars are as instantly memorable as this one and it is still Lamborghini's longest-running nameplate.

The unforgettable Countach had a top speed of 186mph (298km/h).

STREET-LEGAL SALOONS

At a fraction of the cost of many modern supercars, these street-legal saloons ooze just as much panache and attitude. You can see these race-proven, hi-tech, four-wheel drive wonder machines on the streets everyday.

SUBARU IMPREZA WRX STI (2007–)

For those of you who are puzzled at this point, yes, the Impreza is that ordinary four-door family saloon. Except this one, the World Rally Cross version, is a road-legal version of the car that Subaru used to dominate rallying for years. The Japanese company packed all of that competition expertise into the WRX to create a gurgling rally-inspired road rocket that has been around since 1992. A modest 2.5-litre four-cylinder engine gets the turbocharger treatment and belts out 300bhp, enough to take the car to 60mph (97km/h) in 4.8 seconds and on to 155mph (248km/h). With incredible four-wheel-drive handling and more than a healthy dose of spoilers and bodykits, this is the best thing on four-wheels that £26,000 can buy.

The amazing handling of the WRX can embarrass more expensive supercars.

NISSAN GT-R
(2007–)

All the way back in 1989, Nissan reintroduced the name Skyline GT-R to the world. The car was astonishing because boring old Nissan had packed in every latest bit of technology it had and then multiplied it times ten. Four-wheel drive, four-wheel steer, complex electronics that really worked, it was a road and track thoroughbred without a big price tag. With its aggressive styling, everyone loved it and it appeared in the movie *Fast and the Furious* and the *Gran Turismo* Playstation game. The reason for this history lesson? Well the GT-R (now an all-new model and no longer called a Skyline) is still Nissan's top performance machine, punching out 485bhp from its twin-turbo, 3.8-litre, six-cylinder engine. Top speed is 193mph (309km/h) with 0–60mph (97km/h) coming up in just 3.5 seconds. A genuine, one-of-a-kind, supercar crusher – and all for £60,000.

The GT-R has almost 200mph (322km/h) on tap, and brilliant handling.

MITSUBISHI LANCER EVO X
(2008–)

Did we say the Subaru Impreza was the best of its kind? Well hold on, let's not get too carried away here because Mitsubishi have been giving their ordinary family Lancer the same rally treatment since 1992 as well. As its name suggests, this is the tenth version of the car, powered by a 2.0-litre turbocharged engine, producing 440bhp. As with the Subaru, four-wheel drive keeps the car stuck to the road in a way that only a rally-bred car can manage. 0–60mph (97km/h) comes up in a blistering 3.8 seconds – supercar territory – maxing out at 155mph (248km/h). The only slight problem with all of this is the price – £50,000, which almost twice the price of the Subaru WRX…

Few cars can match the Lancer Evo X's rally-bred handling abilities.

THE LAP OF LUXURY

Motoring isn't just about speed and thrills, or even about driving your car yourself. It's also about being whisked to wherever you're going in a car that offers spacious, refined, relaxed comfort. These elite cars and limousines are the ultimate in road luxury.

ROLLS-ROYCE PHANTOM (2003–)

The 'Roller' is the world's most famous luxury brand and the company has been producing its cars since 1906. Now owned by BMW, models come in large or extra large but don't be fooled, these cars aren't just huge sofas on wheels for show-offs. The current Phantom is a beautifully engineered machine, possessing unmatched levels of refinement and comfort. A giant of a car (the extended wheelbase version is the longest standard production car in the world at 240in (6.1m), the tallest at 65in (1.6m) and the heaviest at 6,052lb (2.7 tonnes).
It it is also a very modern version of a traditional British design and it's Rolls-Royce's longest-serving nameplate. Producing 453bhp from its 6.7-litre V12, it can hit 149mph (238km/h), passing 60mph (97km/h) in 5.7 seconds. Step into one and you'll understand why wealthy buyers love them so much – you get to feel like royalty, and that's what it's all about.

The Phantom is the biggest production luxury car from Rolls-Royce.

MAYBACH EXELERO (2005)

If you want to pose, nothing is better than the ultra-rare Exelero.

The outrageous Exelero was stunning. It was a modern version of the streamlined cars that Maybach used to make in the 1930s. But it's hard to imagine it going around a corner or finding a parking spot, because the car is more than 20ft (6m) long. But with 700bhp provided by the twin-turbo V12, 0–60mph (97km/h) comes up in 4.4 seconds, with a top speed of 218mph (349km/h). But none of this really matters because this car is all about enjoying being looked at. Only two of these giants have ever been made but resale values are enormous – one changed hands recently for $8 million (£4.8 million).

'AMERICAN DREAM' LIMOUSINE (2000s)

Not interested in the Rolls-Royces and Maybachs of the world and all that boring tradition? Then how about something a little more custom – a 100ft (33m) purpose-built limo, for example? This amazing machine is the longest car in the world and was built by Hollywood custom car builder Jay Ohrberg. With 24 wheels, there's enough room for a jacuzzi, sun deck, swimming pool, king-sized bed and satellite TV. And if you ever get stuck going around a corner, as you surely will, there's even a helipad at the back so you can be whisked away.

Sometimes only a white limo will do. You can land a helicopter on this one.

THE LAP OF LUXURY

31

The 1980s saw a boom in super fast, outrageously expensive and highly stylised supercars. Within three years, Porsche, Ferrari and Lamborghini had produced era-defining cars that were to rip up the motoring rulebook.

The DMC-12 was the most famous 'could-have-been' story in motoring.

DeLOREAN DMC-12 (1981–83)

John DeLorean was a Detroit car man whose dream was to build his own sports car. The cash he needed curiously came from the British government, who told him that the car had to be made in the UK – Northern Ireland, as it turned out, the first time the country had made a performance car. With its gullwing doors, stainless steel body and futuristic looks the DMC-12 should have been a winner but the recession-hit world of the early 1980s turned its back. But although it looked great, it wasn't much of a performer. It could reach 140mph (224km/h) from its 2.8-litre V6 engine and 0–60mph (97km/h) in 8.8 seconds but these were hardly ground-breaking figures. DeLorean went bust but nevertheless, made famous by the *Back to the Future* films, the DMC-12 will be iconic forever.

PORSCHE 959
(1987-88)

The 959 was the first a new breed of supercar – one that used complex electronics to vastly improve handling. The car could be pushed right up to its 197mph (316km/h) top speed (making it the fastest production car in the world at the time) without any fuss – an incredible achievement at a time when supercars were still difficult to drive. Powered by a twin-turbo, flat-six, 4474cc engine, the 959 bashed out 450bhp and even had four-wheel drive, another first for a supercar, which helped with its blistering 0–62mph (100km/h) time of just 3.7 seconds. Critics thought it a bit soulless, but what no one could deny was that this was the future of fast cars. 330 were made.

TOP 10
FASTEST CARS OF THE 1980s

1	Ferrari F40 – 201mph (322km/h)
2	Porsche 959 – 197mph (316km/h)
3	Ferrari 288 GTO – 189mph (304km/h)
4	Ferrari Testarossa – 180mph (290km/h)
5	Porsche 911 Turbo SE – 171mph (275km/h)
6	Porsche 928 S4 – 168mph (270km/h)
7	Ferrari 328 GTB – 163mph (262km/h)
8	Aston Martin Volante – 162mph (261km/h)
=	Porsche 944 Turbo – 162mph (261km/h)
10	Dodge Viper – 160mph (257km/h)

Porsche created the modern supercar with its world-beating 959.

FERRARI F40
(1987-92)

Ferrari wanted a car to mark its 40th year as a manufacturer and came up with the F40. Head-to-head with the Porsche 959, the F40 was a touch quicker at 201mph (322km/h) and a whole lot more exciting to drive – and dramatic to look at. At the time it was the fastest production car in the world and not surprisingly the most expensive Ferrari money could buy. It was also the last to be signed off by Enzo Ferrari himself. Producing 478bhp from its turbocharged 3-litre V8, 0–60mph (97km/h) came up in 4.5 ear-splitting seconds. You see, Ferrari wanted this car to offer the feel of a real racing car, so it came with a stripped out cabin and no stereo – not that you could have heard one anyway. After an extended production run of 1,200 cars, Ferrari stopped making one of the greatest cars of all time.

Ferrari beat Porsche with the F40, a 201mph (322km/h) classic.

HOW SMALL CAN YOU GO?

If you thought that the Mini or the Fiat 500 were the smallest cars on the road, well, you'd be wrong. Because these were enormous compared to the microcars, which were designed to be the cheapest way of getting behind a steering wheel.

BMW ISETTA (1955-62)

What a cutey. BMW, who had decided to add the tiny Isetta to their range of more usual luxury saloons, got the looks spot on with this 'bubble' car, originally designed by Italian firm Iso. It even had four wheels (although you could have three) and could carry two people, who got in through a front-opening door that brought the steering wheel with it. Powered by a 247–297cc single-cylinder motorcycle engine, it was never going to set speed records on the autobahns but BMW still sold over 160,000 of them, which for a while made the Isetta one of Europe's bestsellers.

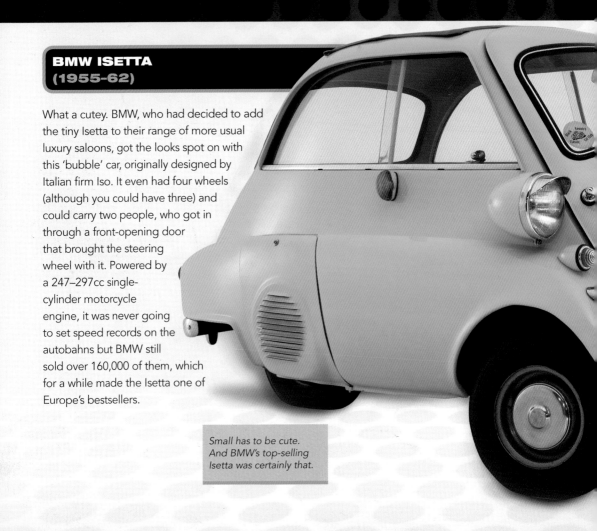

Small has to be cute. And BMW's top-selling Isetta was certainly that.

PEEL P50
(1962-66)

Well there's small, there's micro and then there's the Peel P50. More a toy than a car, this diddy shopping machine was so light it could be picked up and wheeled away. So it's no surprise then that during its lifetime this was the smallest production car available, just 53in (1.3m) long and 39in (99cm) wide. Unfortunately, this three-wheeler was just a single-seater and with only a tiny 49cc single-cylinder engine to power it (the smallest ever put in a production car), it went about the same speed as a toy car did. Only about 100 were ever made yet amazingly it is much loved and is even returned to production in 2010.

The Peel P50 was so small and light you could walk off with it.

TANGO T600
(2005-PRESENT)

Think small means slow? Think again. The firm of Commuter Cars, USA, has built this tiny all-electric car, which will rocket you to 150mph (240km/h), an amazing speed when you consider the car is just 39in (99cm) wide and 101in (257cm) long. It goes without saying that this is the best performing microcar so far. It can carry two people, with the passenger behind the driver, and also boasts lots of comfort, with top models featuring leather trim and a state-of-the-art sound system. George Clooney famously owns one, and if it's good enough for George…

XSK 498

The T600 microcar can hit an extraordinary 150mph (240km/h).

OFF-ROAD RIOTS

Bored with cars that drive on predicable, smooth tarmac? There's plenty of thrills to be had off-road with some extreme machines that are capable of tackling the steepest, roughest tracks in some of the most remote parts the world.

HUMMER H1
(1992-2006)

Like a lot of cars such as this one, the Hummer H1 started life as a military vehicle called the Humvee (check out YouTube videos of it scaling a vertical wall). It is enormous both in how big it is and in its off-road abilities. Over 15ft (4.7m) long and more than 7ft (2.1m) wide, this is not a car to be trifled with. It can wade through nearly 3ft (1m) of water and haul itself up practically any slope. But it is pretty slow, not helped by its bulk. 0–60mph (97km/h) comes up in a leisurely 13.5 seconds and you can't even reach 100mph (160km/h), but these figures are not why you'd want one of these. Indestructible off-road abilities and showing off are.

The Wildcat will blast down a dirt track faster than anything else.

The H1 has a top speed short of 100mph (160km/h) but can tackle most inclines.

BOWLER WILDCAT
(2003-)

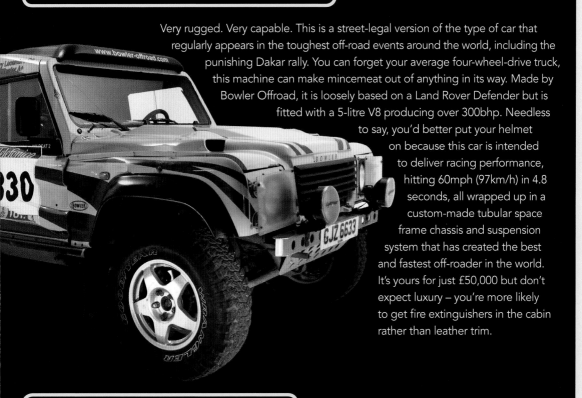

Very rugged. Very capable. This is a street-legal version of the type of car that regularly appears in the toughest off-road events around the world, including the punishing Dakar rally. You can forget your average four-wheel-drive truck, this machine can make mincemeat out of anything in its way. Made by Bowler Offroad, it is loosely based on a Land Rover Defender but is fitted with a 5-litre V8 producing over 300bhp. Needless to say, you'd better put your helmet on because this car is intended to deliver racing performance, hitting 60mph (97km/h) in 4.8 seconds, all wrapped up in a custom-made tubular space frame chassis and suspension system that has created the best and fastest off-roader in the world. It's yours for just £50,000 but don't expect luxury – you're more likely to get fire extinguishers in the cabin rather than leather trim.

THE MARAUDER
(2008-)

OK, so we're cheating a bit. The Marauder is actually a South African 'battlefield taxi'. The only reason it's in this book is because, amazingly, there is a road-legal version of it. You have to wonder why anyone would really need one of these because it is truly massive, one of the biggest four-wheeled road vehicles you can buy. Weighing 9.9 tonnes (21,780lb) it can literally demolish, crush and climb up anything in its path. And it is still armoured and bulletproof, even in civilian form. Despite its bulk it can reach 75mph (120km/h) from its 300bhp engine and has a maximum range of 430 miles (700km), which is just as well because stopping for petrol is not what it does best.

At nearly 10 tonnes, nothing is going to stand in the Marauder's way.

If four wheels just won't do, the extraordinary G63 AMG 6 x 6 is an option.

MERCEDES G63 AMG 6X6
(2013–)

Another vehicle for loonies and show-offs. In case you find that your standard Mercedes G63 SUV isn't good enough off-road, how about sticking a couple more wheels on it to create a 6 x 6, and then get it tuned up by AMG just to make sure you're not being shortchanged in the power output department. This 6 x 6 is a huge double-cab pick-up and like the Marauder, is really a military vehicle converted for civilian use. Powered by a turbocharged 5.5-litre V8 producing 536bhp, this beast can really shift, despite its 3.7 tonne (8,300lb) weight – 0–60mph (97km/h) comes up in less than six seconds, with a top speed limited to 100mph (160km/h). If you really need to drive up a vertical rock face, this is one of the world's most extreme vehicles to do it in – but it's going to cost you £370,000 to buy one.

MONSTER TRUCKS
(1981–)

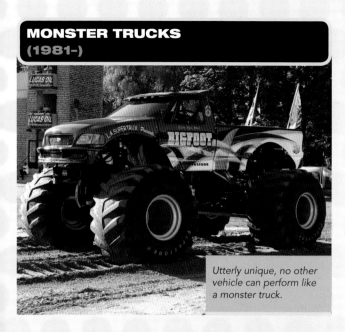

Utterly unique, no other vehicle can perform like a monster truck.

OK, now this is getting silly. Take a 4 x 4 pick-up truck then completely rebuild the suspension so you can add some tyres taken from farm machinery. Then drive up, over and down the other side of anything you like because nothing's going to stop you. The Monster Jam roadshow is the place to see these vehicles in action, bouncing their way around a course of ramps and obstacles. The first monster truck was Bob Chandler's Big Foot, which wowed crowds back in 1981. The trucks (these days, really custom-built dune buggies) are massively strong and weigh at least four tonnes (9,000lb). No wonder then that they are powered by 9-litre engines running on alcohol. A truly unique sight in the world of motoring.

FORMULA OFFROAD
(PRESENT)

If you live in Iceland, which has lots of very steep mountains made out of volcanic ash, what better way to spend a Saturday afternoon than attempting to drive your insanely powerful custom dune buggy to the top of one? Increasingly popular all over the Nordic countries, extreme hillclimbing like this has to be seen to be believed, not least because hardly anyone ever makes it to the top before toppling over backwards, wrecking their car in the process. And if that doesn't take your fancy, how about driving on water? The tyres on these buggies are so wide and spin so fast you can actually aquaplane your way across a lake. Buggies are often powered by turbocharged V8 engines with nitro boost, producing over 1,000bhp. Put that power through a four-wheel drive system with paddle tyres and you've got a car that can quite literally fly, or drive, on water!

Formula Offroad buggies are the most extreme hillclimbers in the world.

COOL CARS OF THE 1990s

By the time the 1990s rolled around, the manufacturing contest between Ferrari and Porsche went off the boil as yet another recession dented car sales. But by the mid-90s the pace was higher than ever and some new players had appeared, all selling hi-tech exotica for ever bigger sums of money.

LAMBORGHINI DIABLO (1990–2001)

Replacing that 1970s and 80s classic, the Countach, was always going to be a tall order but Lamborghini pulled it off with the Diablo, hiring Marcello Gandini again to design the bodywork. His creation was another wedge: wide, low and sleek. Job done, this car was a riot to drive and to look at. Producing up to 525bhp out of its 5.7-litre V12, it was the fastest production car of its time, hitting 207mph (331km/h) and reaching 0–60mph (97km/h) in 3.7 seconds, enough to push your eyeballs back into your head. The Diablo (meaning 'devil' in Italian) also had scissor doors, making it one of the coolest cars to seen posing in.

TOP 10 FASTEST CARS OF THE 1990s

1	McLaren F1	240mph (386km/h)
2	Ferrari F50	234mph (377km/h)
3	Bugatti EB110	217mph (349km/h)
4	Jaguar XJ220	213mph (343km/h)
5	Lamborghini Diablo	207mph (331km/h)
6	Aston Martin Vantage 600	200mph (322km/h)
=	Mercedes CLK GTR	200mph (322km/h)
8	Ferrari 550 Maranello	199mph (320km/h)
9	Ferrari 512 M	196mph (315km/h)
10	Dodge Viper GTS	190mph (306km/h)

The Diablo was the fastest car in the world in its day, at 207mph (331km/h).

JAGUAR XJ220
(1992-94)

Just when Lamborghini, Ferrari and Porsche thought they had it all wrapped up, along comes another challenger. The XJ220 (the 220 referred to its intended top speed in miles per hour) became the world's fastest production car in 1992, hitting a whopping 213mph (343km/h). Its twin-turbo V6 produced 542bhp and rocketed the car to 62mph (100km/h) in 3.9 seconds. Although the car was amazing to look at, it was big and poor visibility out of the cabin made it hard to drive. With a price of £470,000, Jaguar couldn't even sell the 275 cars it had made. What a shame.

The XJ220 was once the fastest car in the world, at 213mph (343km/h).

McLAREN F1
(1994-98)

Where Jaguar stumbled with the XJ220, McLaren succeeded magnificently with the F1. The best-ever supercar in many people's eyes, it is still the fastest-ever normally aspirated car. McLaren, of course, are an F1 racing team, and they put all their know-how into their new road car. Producing 627bhp from a purpose-built BMW 6-litre V12, the F1 became yet another 'fastest car in the world' as it hit 240mph (386km/h), with 0–60mph (97km/h) coming up in a body-squashing 3.2 seconds. The first production car to use a full carbon fibre monocoque chassis, it is the only three-seater supercar ever, with the driver in the middle. The price was a bit off-putting, though – £635,000 was an eye-watering amount and only 100 cars were ever made.

20 years old, the F1 is still regarded as one of the best supercars ever made.

PUT THAT IN YOUR TANK!

Petrol (or gasoline as it's called in America) is the drink of choice for your car. And generally, along with it's grubbier cousin diesel, it's an excellent source of energy. But that hasn't stopped car designers from trying different fuels and engines.

GENERAL MOTORS FIREBIRD II (1956)

In 1950, British car company Rover unveiled the JET1 gas turbine powered car, powered by the same kind of engine to be found in a jet fighter of the time. What a great idea – fighter jet performance in a car! Unfortunately, what worked on an aeroplane wouldn't scale down very easily to a car. The turbine itself powered the car to 88mph (140km/h) but spun at 50,000rpm, guzzling fuel and making the cabin very hot. Several US car companies had a go at the same idea, including General Motors, who in 1956 produced the Firebird II, complete with its fantastic jet fighter looks. Futuristic to the core, the designers wanted the car to be controlled by a computer and to steer itself – and they just about managed it, a marvel for the time. But it was all too experimental and old-fashioned engines, powered by old-fashioned petrol, won out.

The Firebird II tried to use jet engine technology in a car but it was all too much.

The Nucleon was going to be powered by a nuclear reactor – be afraid!

FORD NUCLEON
(1958)

We all know about the incredible amounts of energy produced during nuclear reactions. We all know that it can be used to power military submarines and aircraft carriers. So why not put a bit in your car as well? During the atomic age of the 1950s, Ford toyed with the idea. After all, what could possibly go wrong? Luckily for us, the idea never went any further than a scale model or else every car crash would have unleashed a mini-Armageddon in the street. As if the idea wasn't barmy enough, the design of the car itself, with its vast over-hanging nose, had accident written all over it. Let's just call this one a flight of fancy.

TOP FUEL DRAGSTER
(PRESENT)

Top Fuel dragsters are easily the fastest racing cars of any kind. They hurtle down a 1,000ft (300m) drag strip with a blaze of flames leaping from the exhausts. 0–60mph (97km/h) comes up in just over half a second. The race itself lasts less than four seconds as they cross the finishing line at a staggering 330mph (530km/h). So how is this performance possible? The answer isn't actually to be found in the size of the engine but in the type of fuel it uses – nitromethane, mixed with some methanol. It quite literally turns the engine into a 10,000bhp bomb.

Nothing accelerates like this. 0–60mph (97km/h) takes about half a second.

PEOPLE'S CARS

After World War II, Europe needed small, affordable cars to get its population on the move again. Despite tiny engines and few creature comforts, these cars became much-loved classics that had sales figures measured in the tens of millions. They also made bigger, faster cars look heavy and clumsy.

VW BEETLE (1945-78)

This might just be the world's most famous car. Although design was started during World War II, production really got going in 1945. Despite its low price, this was a well-made car that was exported everywhere, mostly to the American market, which took the Beetle to it heart. Everybody loved the cute looks and distinctive engine noise, made by its flat-four rear-mounted unit. By the time the last of the German-made cars was completed in 1978, worldwide sales stood at 21 million cars and it was the company's longest serving nameplate.

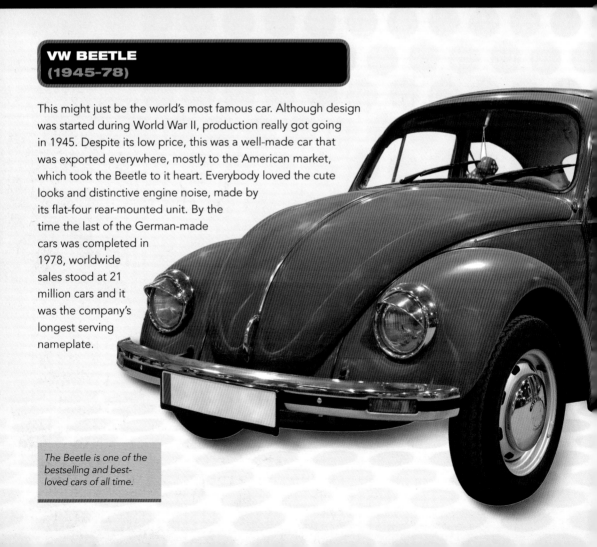

The Beetle is one of the bestselling and best-loved cars of all time.

The tiny 500 was cute, cheap and an true icon of Italian car design.

FIAT 500
(1957-75)

TOP 10
BESTSELLING CARS

1	Toyota Corolla (1966–present)	40 million
2	Ford F-Series (1948–present)	34 million
3	VW Golf (1974–present)	25 million
4	VW Beetle (1945–78)	21 million
5	Vaz-2101 (1970–88)	19 million
6	Ford Model T (1908–27)	15 million
7	Fiat Uno (1983–2004)	9 million
8	Renault Clio (1991–present)	9 million
9	Mini (1959–2000)	5.5 million
10	Hindustan Ambassador (1958–present)	4 million

This was the car put Italy on wheels. A little gem, it was tiny and originally only had a 0.5-litre, flat-twin engine in the back. Despite a top speed of only 55mph (88km/h), no one was bothered as they were too busy enjoying the go-kart handling and the full-length sunroof that came on early models. With total sales of four million, this was truly a people's car.

The bestselling British car of all time, the Mini is a icon of the Swinging Sixties.

MINI
(1959-2000)

The original Mini was around for so long that it seems hard to imagine a time when it wasn't. The car that took Britain into the Swinging Sixties was a masterpiece of design – despite its size, it made fantastic use of every square inch of interior space. It was also great to drive and was powered by a variety of front-mounted, four-cylinder engines, from 850–1275cc. The Mini quickly became fashionable and successful, with a vast number of different models – including vans, pick-ups and race-winning 'Cooper' editions – racking up worldwide sales of over 5.5 million cars. This made it the most popular British car ever made. A "retro redesign" of the original Mini was launched by BMW in 2001.

HYPERCAR HEAVEN

Exactly when supercars started becoming hypercars is open to debate. But from these machines you can see how performance cars started to become more and more extreme in every way. And crucially, their posing value is even higher than their top speeds!

FERRARI ENZO (2002-03)

One problem with Ferrari is that as soon as they've finished building their 'ultimate' supercar, they then start building another one, even more 'ultimate' than the last. How are we to keep up? The Enzo was the result of Project FX, the car designed to replace the F50. Carrying the name of the man who started the company might have put everyone under pressure, but Ferrari pulled off something really spectacular. A 6.0-litre V12 pushed the car along to 218mph (349km/h) after reaching 60mph (97km/h) in under 3.2 seconds. The carbon fibre 'tub' chassis, bespoke Brembo brakes and F1-style paddle gearbox made this the most exciting Ferrari ever made. Only 400 left the factory, with the last one, oddly, going to Pope John Paul II. An even more extreme track day car based on the Enzo, the FXX, came later, with a limited production run of just 30 cars.

The Enzo was pure genius and was able to hit 218mph (349km/h).

PORSCHE CARRERA GT
(2004-07)

This has to be the first time a 200mph (322km/h) car has been made by accident. Having cancelled some racing development work, Porsche thought they may as well stick their research in a concept car to see if anyone liked it. Everyone loved it and the car went into production. Powered by a 5.7-litre V10 engine producing 612bhp, it could hit 60mph (97km/h) in under four seconds on its way to its 205mph (328km/h) top speed. The car also didn't have any electronic driver aids. This was a real drivers cars and is regarded as one of the most exciting car Porsche has ever made.

The Carrera GT was one of the original hypercars and a true driver's car.

The Sesto Elemento is Lamborghini's carbon-fibre masterpiece.

LAMBORGHINI SESTO ELEMENTO
(2011)

The material of choice for building hypercars these days is carbon fibre. Most companies build their chassis out of it, but Lamborghini have uniquely made this entire car out of it. So much so in fact that the car's name translates as 'sixth element', which in the periodic table, is carbon. So what does all this carbon fibre get you? A car that weighs less than 1,000kg (2,200lb) for starters, which is unheard of on a machine like this, making it the lightest car Lamborghini has ever made. It's also very strong. And very expensive. And very exclusive. Just 20 were made, for track use only, costing up to $2.9 million (£1.7 million). Of course all were sold. Power comes from a 5.2-litre V10 engine borrowed from the Gallardo, generating 570bhp, which in car this light gives extraordinary performance. Lamborghini claims a 0–62mph (0–100km/h) time of 2.5 seconds and a top speed of well over 200mph (322km/h).

SALEEN S7 TWIN TURBO
(2007-09)

The Saleen was America's first production hypercar and could belt out 220mph (356km/h) without too much bother from its monster Ford 7-litre V8. But this was a naturally aspirated engine – meaning that its makers just couldn't resist bolting a couple of turbos onto it to see what might happen. Well, guess what? They created one of the fastest cars ever made. Power output was raised to 750bhp, which boosted top speed to a mind-blowing 248mph (399km/h) – Bugatti Veyron territory. 0–60mh (97km/h) came up in 2.8 seconds. Very few car makers have ever produced anything quite like this.

The S7 Twin Turbo was one of the fastest cars ever made.

PORSCHE 911 GT2 RS (2010)

It's amazing to think that the classic 911 has been around since 1963 and it is Porsche's longest-serving nameplate. Since then it has undergone several upgrades under the skin, but outwardly it is still recognizable as the company's bestselling supercar – an incredible 820,000 cars up to 2013. Of course, it has got faster and faster and in 2010 Porsche decided to raise the bar again. They were already selling the great GT2, but why not put it on a diet, losing 150lb (72kg), and increase power by about 90bhp? Along with the Carrera GT, the result was the most powerful petrol-driven Porsche ever made. Pushing out 612bhp from its twin-turbo 3.6-litre flat-six engine, the car can hit 62mph (100km/h) in 3.4 seconds and has a top speed of 205mph (330km/h). And all of this in a rear-wheel drive format, making it one of the most extreme and demanding driving experiences to come out of Porsche's factory in Stuttgart.

The 911 GT2 RS was massively fast and extreme in every way.

TOP 10 FASTEST CARS

1	SSC Tuatara – 276mph (444km/h)*
2	SSC Ultimate Aero TT – 271mph (436km/h)*
3	Koenigsegg Agera R – 270mph (435km/h)*
4	Hennessey Venom GT – 270mph (435km/h)*
5	Bugatti Veyron Super Sport – 268mph (415km/h)
6	Bugatti Veyron – 254mph (408km/h)
7	Saleen S7 Twin Turbo – 248mph (399km/h)
8	McLaren F1 – 240mph (386km/h)
9	Pagani Huayra – 231mph (372km/h)
10	Noble M600 – 225mph (362km/h)

* claimed

VIP MOTORS

These are the cars for people who are very special. In fact, you have to be so special that these cars get made specially for you. Exactly what type of car you get in depends on what you do. Some are designed to hide you away, while others are designed to show you off to as many people as possible.

ZIL LIMOUSINE
(1936-87)

Russian company Zil has been making cars, trucks and buses since 1916 but it is most famous for the black limousines it made for Soviet top brass. Ironically, one of the earliest examples from the 1940s is rumoured to have been based on an American Packard Super Eight. Whatever, several models followed during the Communist era, each one as huge and gloomy as the last. The final version, the Zil-4104, had a 7.7-litre V8 engine, with a claimed 311bhp. This could manage over 100mph (160km/h) and was, during the model's lifetime, one of the world's biggest production-car engines. The Zil limousine has become a motoring icon of the Soviet era, though during its heyday ordinary Russians were well advised to stay out of the way of this car – and anyone travelling inside it.

The huge Zil limousine was the ride of choice for top-level Soviet officials.

POPEMOBILE
(1976-)

The Pope is a man who needs to be seen by his flock and can't hide himself away in an armoured limo. Instead, his Popemobile is designed to make him as visible as possible to the crowds who come to see him. A very unique vehicle, there have been lots of Popemobile designs over the years, starting with a converted Toyota Landcruiser in 1976. These early cars were open air, but after the attempted assassination of Pope John Paul II in 1981, most now have a closed canopy. The current car is an amour-plated Mercedes-Benz M-Class SUV. But Popemobiles are not all top-heavy white cars clad in bullet-proof glass. In 1988, Pope John Paul II toured the Ferrari factory in Italy. His ride? A Ferrari Mondiale – the Cabriolet version, so he could stand up.

There have been a number of different Popmobile designs.

CADILLAC ONE 'THE BEAST'
(2009)

This is the car that carts around the most important man in the world – the American President. This state car, sometimes called Limo One (to match the President's Airforce One plane) is a one-off design and has features straight out of a James Bond film. Designed to shrug off any attack short of nuclear explosion it has 8in (20cm) thick armour plating, 5in (13cm) thick bulletproof glass, night vision and run-flat tyres. The car is also sealed against biochemical attacks and has its own oxygen supply. Along with a small arsenal of weapons in the boot there is also a store of the President's blood for emergency transfusions. Needless to say, it's not called The Beast for nothing. Weighing around nine tonnes, 0–60mph (97km/h) takes about 15 seconds. 60mph (97km/h) is also its top speed. And try not to laugh when you see it attempting corners.

'The Beast' is the most heavily protected car in the world.

SUPERCARS OF THE 2000s

By the start of the 21st century, supercars were highly sophisticated machines. Gone were the old difficult-to-drive beasts and lots of electronic aids became the norm. These allowed drivers to squeeze out every last bit of performance from these amazing machines.

ASTON MARTIN V12 VANTAGE (2007–)

The original Vantage was a great-looking car but 'only' had a V8 engine in it. Clearly this wasn't enough for some people, so Aston Martin managed to wedge a mighty V12, borrowed from the DBS, into the car instead. The result? Fireworks would be the word. Underneath the beautiful styling the Aston, always poised, always cool, always luxurious, raced all the way to 190mph (304km/h) via a 0–60mph (97km/h) time of 4.1 seconds. The 'S' version, announced in 2013, gives even more thrills, taking power up to 565bhp from an all-new 6.0 litre engine. This allows the car to race all the way up to 205mph (330km/h), making it the fastest production Aston Martin on the road.

Nothing touches the V12 Vantage for civilized driving thrills. It is superb.

LAMBORGHINI LP670-4SV
(2009-10)

The SV bit at the end of the name of this car stands for Super Veloce – super fast. It's true to say that Lambo went to town with this version of the Murcielago, creating the ultimate charging bull. It was also very big and the fastest car the company had made at the time, all wrapped up in styling that only Lamborghini could pull off. 661bhp from a 6.5-litre V12 powered this beast all the way to 212mph (339km/h), passing 60mph (97km/h) in just 2.8 seconds. The cabin was small and the scissor doors were hard to live with, but no one cared, it was stunning. 186 people got to buy one.

Lambo make extreme cars and the LP670-4SV ticked all the boxes.

AUDI R8
(2007-)

The Audi R8 is a real cracker. Pushed along (from 2008) by a 4.2-litre V10 engine and four-wheel drive, this German mean machine has a top speed beyond 190mph (304mph). It has the kind of road manners that leave you completely unruffled and it looked really cool, too, scooping all sorts of awards when it first came out. More than 50,000 have been made, which means it isn't very exclusive, but buyers were too busy enjoying driving theirs to care.

The R8 looked brilliant and had the handling to match. It is a real favourite.

IS THAT A GOOD IDEA?

The world of cars is full of really cool designs that everyone loves and that will be talked about and admired forever. It's also full of ideas that looked good on paper but didn't work. Or that turned out to be the wrong car at the wrong time. Or were just plain barmy in the first place.

DYMAXION III
(1934)

Designed by an American engineer called Buckminster Fuller, the Dymaxion III was an attempt to create a people carrier using ideas and materials borrowed from the aircraft industry. This was a great idea and his streamlined machine looked light years ahead of any other vehicle on the road at the time. It placed the passengers at the front and a Ford V8 at the back but it was a three-wheeler, with an huge overhang at the front, so it couldn't get around corners very well. Fuller also made wild claims about its performance – he said 0–60mph (97km/h) took three seconds and top speed was 120mph (193km/h). When a prototype crashed, this experimental car was destined to remain just that.

The unique Dymaxion III borrowed ideas from the aircraft industry.

RELIANT ROBIN
(1973-2002)

The Robin always looked like it was going to roll over but it was cheap.

The Robin appeared in the early 1970s and has been the butt of countless jokes. However, there is a reason why it exists. For starters, having only three wheels means in Britain, at least, it is technically a motorbike, and so owners have to pay less tax. It is also very light so you don't need a full licence to drive it. All of which makes sense for low-budget motorists. Unfortunately that's where the positives end. For starters, having a single wheel at the front always made it look like it was going to topple over. And it was very slow and ugly. The 'Plastic Pig', as it was nicknamed, had a 0–60mph (97km/h) time of 16.1 seconds and power output from it tiny 850cc engine was just 40bhp, all providing a top speed of 85mph (136km/h). Nevertheless, the Robin continues to have a loyal fan club.

The Panther 6 was unique and could hit a claimed 200mph (322km/h).

PANTHER 6
(1977-78)

If you think this car looks like something out of the *Thunderbirds*, well, it does. F1 team Tyrrell had shown that a six-wheel racing car could work on the track, so why shouldn't that idea be brought to road cars? And at the same time, why not make it one of the most incredibly powerful cars of its era? Powered by a twin-turbo 8.2-litre V8 engine from a Cadillac, this mighty beast claimed a top speed of 200mph (322km/h), though no one was ever brave enough to test that out. It was luxurious and hi-tech as well, with a spec list that included electronic instruments, air conditioning, electric seats and windows, a phone and even a TV. All of which seemed to confuse rather than attract buyers and the car was a flop. Just two examples of this unique car were made.

MOVIE MACHINES

From Bond to Batman and from Minis to Mustangs, the big screen is the perfect place to show off amazing cars, driven by the coolest actors. And it's often the car that turns out to be the star.

The most beautiful Aston Martin ever made? James Bond loved his.

ASTON MARTIN DB5 – *GOLDFINGER* (1964)

This was the car that started it all for James Bond, and his history of great cars all loaded up with amazing gadgets can be traced back to this 1964 Aston Martin DB5 (which also appears in *Thunderball*, a year later). The long list of weapons and gizmos loaded into the car included machine guns, an ejector seat, a smoke screen, a bulletproof shield and a navigation system that wouldn't look out of place on a modern car. The original car would have made an excellent machine for a chase because it was fast. Its 4-litre six-cylinder engine produced 282bhp, good enough for 145mph (233km/h), a very impressive figure. And it looked beautiful too – for many the best Aston Martin ever made.

The only thing cooler than Steve McQueen was his Mustang GT 390.

FORD MUSTANG GT 390 –
BULLITT (1968)

One of the world's most iconic actors, Steve McQueen's performance as Frank Bullitt in the 1968 thriller is one of the most enthralling, super-cool pieces of acting ever. However, he was always in danger of being upstaged by his mechanical co-star – Ford's Mustang GT 390 Fastback muscle car. Not that McQueen would have minded – he was a car fanatic himself and fell in love the Mustang. The 320bhp produced by the Mustang came from a 6.4-litre V8 which could take the car to 130mph (210km/h), after reaching 60mph (97km/h) in 6.2 seconds. All of which was used to create one the greatest car chases in movie history, through the hilly streets of San Francisco.

VW BEETLE –
THE LOVE BUG (1968)

Herbie was the Beetle with the cute personality and everyone loved him.

This was the film that first introduced the world to Herbie, the car with a mind all of his own. The film, and its four sequels, were massive hits with younger audiences – the combination of gentle comedy and a cute car with a mischievous personality was just right. Herbie was a 1963 VW Beetle, apparently chosen by Disney, the studio that made the film, because during casting it was the only car that made the crew want to pet it. Herbie carries the racing number '53' and could always be relied on to save the day, though with a real top speed of about 70mph (113km/h) from a 1200cc engine, he wouldn't have been that much of a racer.

MINI COOPER S –
THE ITALIAN JOB (1969)

The Mini Cooper S showed what a brilliant car it was in The Italian Job.

One of the great British crime capers, the film is famous for its super-cool Cockney gangster played by Michael Caine, its appearance from playwright Noel Coward and Mini Coopers. Loaded with stolen gold, the cars have to escape the traffic jam deliberately created by Caine and his gang to delay the police. The chase scene in the film, where three Coopers, painted red, white and blue, race down pavements, stairs and through sewer pipes, gradually shrugging off the police in their slow and clumsy cars is one of the greats – a sort of urban rallying designed to show off the incredible handling and sparky performance the Mini Cooper was loved for. This came as no surprise to motorsport fans of the time – the Cooper S, which appeared in 1963, had already won the Monte Carlo rally in 1964, '65 and '67. It was the best performance small car of its time.

Bond's cool Esprit was the perfect car for his underwater adventure.

LOTUS ESPRIT S1 –
THE SPY WHO LOVED ME (1976)

Bond, as we all know, loves his cars. Aston Martins, Cadillacs, BMWs, Jaguars, it doesn't really matter so long as it looks cool, goes fast, has lots of gadgets and has the firepower to shoot down a helicopter. Which leads us neatly onto a certain Lotus Esprit, which could drive into the sea and turn into a fantastic submersible. It also had ferocious weaponry, as witnessed by the missile it launches from beneath the waves to destroy the baddies' helicopter hovering above. When the car drives out of the sea, astonishing the sunbathers on the beach, movie audiences started applauding. The 134mph (216km/h) Series 1 Esprit, which appeared in 1975, was a great car, whose crisp, modern styling looked just the part. Who would have thought it would make such a great submarine, too?

BATMOBILE TUMBLER –
THE DARK KNIGHT TRILOGY (2005-12)

If Bond had standard road cars adapted for him, Batman went one step further and built his own Batmobile. The 'old' iconic Batmobile that featured on the 1960s TV series started life as a 1955 Lincoln Futura concept car – with a rocket thruster for making fast starts, of course. Then the supersonic-jet-engine-on-wheels styling for *Batman* and *Batman Returns* (1989 and 1992) became Batman's ride. But it's the tough, military-style Tumbler from *Batman Begins* (2005) and *The Dark Knight* (2012) that is the one to watch now. Powered by a big Chevrolet V8, this is a serious piece of kit, with 0–60mph (97km/h) coming up 5 seconds. Add on some chunky 37in (94cm) tyres, lots of carbon fibre and a massive suspension system and you've got yourself a car fit for a hero.

The Batmobile was always fast but the Tumbler is now also tough.

CAR, BOAT OR PLANE?

For decades bumpy, uneven and congested roads have limited the fun you can have in four wheels. Not anymore! When it comes to the future of global car manufacturing, the sea, and sky, is the limit!

GIBBS AQUADA (2003-04)

If you could drive your car all the way to the coast and then just press a button and your car could turn into a proper boat, would that be a good idea? Gibbs Sports Amphibians, the people behind the Aquada, certainly thought so. And they made it work really well, too. The Aquada used a 2.5-litre V6 engine from a Land Rover Freelander and drove reasonably well on land, even topping 100mph (160km/h). But it was in the water where it worked best, hitting 30mph (48km/h) with its jet ski propulsion. However for the £150,000 asking price you could have bought yourself a proper car and a proper boat, and have lots of change left over as well. Nevertheless this was a serious piece of engineering and is regarded as one of the best amphibious cars ever built.

The Aquada could even fold its wheels up clear of the water.

aquada

Being able to turn your car into a submarine is the ultimate showstopper.

RINSPEED SQUBA (2008)

Rinspeed took the Aquada idea one step further and turned their car into a submersible. Using the chassis from a Lotus Elise, the sQuba (complete with a capital Q) was all-electric and could cruise on land at 75mph (120km/h) and underwater at 2mph (3km/h). Watching the car 'fly' underwater was an impressive sight but there was one snag – there was no roof, meaning that as soon as you were in the water, you were soaked. In fact, you would have drowned without the built-in scuba-diving equipment. Nevertheless, this was the only car in the world that would allow you to reinact that famous car-drives-out-of-the-sea-and-onto-the-beach scene from the James Bond movie *The Spy Who Loved Me*.

TERRAFUGIA TRANSITION (PRESENT)

The Transition might just turn out to be the best flying car ever created.

Getting a car to sprout wings and take off is extremely difficult and inventors have been wrestling with the idea for years. Perhaps though, the Terrafugia Transition could change all that. This odd-looking machine, with its wings folded up like a bat while in car mode, is never going to be all that great on the motorway, though the inventors do claim a 70mph (120km/h) top speed. But its the plane bit they really have to get right and a working prototype does exist, with a 107mph (172km/h) cruising speed and a range of 489 miles (787km). Not bad, eh? This is the best-engineered flying car around and it might just go into full production.

THE FUTURE

It is always difficult predicting the future. But if current trends continue, the future of the car is very much electric. Already petrol-electric hybrids are becoming the norm and as battery technology improves, does this spell the end of the internal combustion engine?

MERCEDES-BENZ SLS AMG ED (2013–)

Just because the future is electric does not mean the future is slow and boring. Quite the opposite. Enter the SLS AMG Electric Drive. It does everything its petrol-powered sister does (that is, provide stunning looks and supercar performance) but better, because it has even more power. Four electric motors, one on each wheel, power the car and develop a total of 740bhp, that's 118bhp more than the petrol version. 0–62mph (100km/h) comes up in 3.9 seconds and top speed is limited to 155mph (248km/h). As normal though, there are a couple of small points. The batteries are a bit heavy so the car weighs more than two tonnes (4,400lb). Range is about 160 miles (250km) which isn't bad but recharging is still slow. And then there's the price – at over £330,000 it ain't cheap. And of course, it's all a bit quiet in the exhaust department. But this is by far the best electric supercar around.

The SLS AMG ED can hit 62mph (100km/h) in just 3.9 seconds.

BMW i3
(2013–)

How about an electric car that's now in production, doesn't cost a fortune, looks great and is made by one of the world's best motor manufacturers? How about the BMW i3? So far, everyone loves it. Power comes from a battery-powered motor producing 170bhp and since keeping weight down is important on electric cars, the i3 is the first car of its type to have most of its internal structure and body made of carbon fibre reinforced plastic. A range of 120 miles (200km) will keep most people happy around town but just in case, there is also a 'range extender' option. This adds a 650cc petrol engine, which acts as a generator to charge the batteries. Expect other manufacturers to follow suit.

The i3's 120-mile (200km) range is great for most urban commutes.

VW XL1
(2013–)

If the all-electric idea doesn't quite appeal, there's always the hybrid, and there are a few of these around, including the bestselling Toyota Prius. And while these cars do still burn petrol (or diesel), they are hardly gas guzzlers. VW are making 250 examples of what is now the world's most fuel-efficient car, managing a staggering 313mpg. The whole car only weighs 795kg (1,749lb), mostly because large chunks of it are made out of carbon fibre, which helps boost its economy. An 800cc diesel engine helps the electric motor and the whole package is wrapped up in an incredibly streamlined body that makes sure that you'll not be spending much time or cash in petrol stations.

VW's XL1 is the world's most fuel-efficient car, capable of 313mpg.

PICTURE CREDITS

The publishers would like to thank the following sources for their kind permission to reproduce the pictures in this book.

1. © Ferrari, 3. Shutterstock/Sam Moores, 4t. © Porsche, 4b Corbis/Hennessey/Splash News, 5t. Shutterstock/Max Earey, 5b. © Ferrari, 6-7. © Daimler. All Rights Reserved, 7t. © Rolls-Royce Enthusiasts Club, 7b National Motor Museum/Heritage Images/Getty Images, 8 Keystone-France/Gamma-Keystone via Getty Images, 9t Corbis/Martyn Goddard, 9b Car Culture/Corbis, 10 Shutterstock/Max Earey & 11b. Shutterstock/Pan Xunbin, 11t djandyw.com, 12t © Pagani Automobili S.p.A,, 12b Shutterstock/Max Earey , 13. Hennessey/Splash News/Corbis, 14. © Ariel, 15t © Caterham, 15b. Patrick T. Fallon/Bloomberg via Getty Images, 16. © Daimler. All Rights Reserved, 17t Rex/Magic Car Pics, 17b Rex/Evo, 18t National Motor Museum/Heritage Images/Getty Images, 18b John Lamm/Transtock/Corbis, 19. Rex/Magic Car Pics, 20-21. Phil Talbot/Alamy, 21t. © Rich Niewiroski Jr., 21b. © Magnus Manske, 22. © Porsche, 23t © Norbert Aepli, 23b. & 24. © Ferrari, 25t. ravas51, 25b © Lamborghini, 26. Motoring Picture Library/Alamy, 27t. © Car Culture/Corbis , 27b. Tom Wood/Alamy, 28. © Subaru, 29t. Shutterstock/Teddy Leung, 29b © Mitsubishi, 30. Motoring Picture Library/Alamy, 31t. Maybach-Motorenbau GmbH (Daimler AG), 31b. Maureen Donaldson/Michael Ochs Archives/Getty Images, 32c. Transtock/Corbis, 32-33b. Rex/Magic Car Pics, 33t. Motoring Picture Library/Alamy, 34-35. Rex/Magic Car Pics, 35t Central Press/Hulton Archive/Getty Images, 35b. D0li0, 36. Alan Schein Photography/Corbis, 37t. Rex/Magic Car Pics, 37b. Paramountgroup.biz, 38. Toshifumi Kitamura/AFP/Getty Images, 39t. Shutterstock/Maksim Shmeljov, 40. Shutterstock/Christoff, 41t. Rex/Magic Car Pics, 41b. Motoring Picture Library/Alamy, 42. Bettmann/Corbis, 43t. Private Collection, 43b. Mike Fuentes/Fort Worth Star-Telegram/MCT via Getty Images, 44. Shutterstock/Rob Wilson, 44t. Shutterstock/Catarina Belova, 44c. Shutterstock/JazzBoo, 46. Rex/Magic Car Pics, 47t. Shutterstock/Max Earey, 47c. Shutterstock/Olga Besnard, 48. Shutterstock/Adam Middleton, 49. © Porsche, 50. Rex/Peter Brooker, 51t. Rex/Stephen Simpson, 51b. US Secret Service, 52. © Aston Martin, 53t. Rex/Action Press, 53b. Shutterstock/Kosarev Alexander, 54. Bettmann/Corbis, 55t. Rex/Magic Car Pix, 55c Private Collection, 56. @ Aston Martin, 57t The Kobal Collection/Warner Bros, 57b Rex/Moviestore Collection, 58. Rex/Courtesy Everett Collection, 59t. Allstar Picture Library/Alamy, 59b. Pictorial Press Ltd/Alamy, 60 Rex/Magic Car Pics, 61t. Courtesy of Rinspeed, 61b. Terrafugia Inc., 62. © Daimler AG Mercedes-Benz, 63t. Shutterstock/Fingerhut, 63b. © Volkswagen, 64. © Porsche

Every effort has been made to acknowledge correctly and contact the source and/or copyright holder of each picture and Carlton Books Limited apologises for any unintentional errors or omissions, which will be corrected in future editions of this book.